# A Vision for Change
## How to Help Someone With Addiction or Mental Illness

Melissa Deuter, MD
Rich Whitman

Copyright © 2019 by Melissa Deuter, MD and Richard Whitman. All rights reserved

This book, or parts thereof may not be reproduced in any form without permission from the publishers except for brief excerpts used for reviews.

Published by Melissa Deuter, MD and Richard Whitman.

ISBN 13: 978-1-937985-58-5

ISBN 10: 1-937985-58-X

Printed in the U.S.A.

The information in this book is meant to offer advice and share clinical experience based on the authors' work with families and significant others who love someone facing addiction or mental illness. This book is not intended as a substitute for any medical advice or professional advice about any specific experience or situation. As each situation is different, supportive loved ones should seek the advice of their own physician or medical professional.

# About The Author

Richard (Rich) Whitman, with over 30 years of experience, is a trusted interventionist and respected leader in the field of addiction recovery. A pioneer in the industry, Rich has been instrumental in building some of the finest treatment programs in the nation and served as a primary treatment advisor to Dr. Phil McGraw for eight seasons of the Dr. Phil show. Rich is an Independent Consultant and the Founder of Whitman Recovery Service. In this role, he provides maximum service to hundreds of individuals and their families every year to access the best treatment options available.

Rich is a Nationally Certified Intervention Professional. He has successfully conducted well over 500 interventions throughout the United States and has made numerous television appearances. Rich combines decades of clinical expertise with a no-nonsense style that quickly gains the trust of clients and families alike. He is professional, compassionate, and dedicated to help every individual and family struggling with addictive disorders.

Melissa Deuter, MD is a board-certified psychiatrist and founder of Sigma Mental Health Urgent Care based in San Antonio, Texas. Dr. Deuter currently holds an appointment as Clinical Assistant Professor in the Department of Psychiatry at University of Texas Health Science Center at San Antonio, where she is actively involved in clinical research, teaching seminars, and supervising the work of medical students and psychiatry residents. She is a current member of the Texas Society of Psychiatric Physicians Ethics Council, and a current member of the South Texas Psychiatric Physicians Research Network's Executive Committee.

Dr. Deuter has been recognized repeatedly for her clinical work and has been named a "Top Doctor" and a "Best of" Doctor as well as a Texas Super Doctor's "Rising Star." She also has received the American Registry "Patient's Choice Award." Dr. Deuter has a special interest in early-stage psychiatric care, differentiating serious illness from normal brain development and serving the unique mental health needs of emerging adults. She is a regular blogger and the author of STUCK in the Sick Role: How Illness Becomes an Identity.

# Table of Contents

**Part 1 Mental Disorders, Addictions, and Insight "There's nothing wrong with me!"** .................. 1

Mental Health and Insight ................................................. 3

Addiction and Denial ....................................................... 11

**Part 2 How the System Tries (and Fails) to Help** ..... 21

Finding Help in a Broken System ...................................... 23

Finding Help at Last ......................................................... 26

Your Loved One Found Help. Now What? ...................... 34

What Your Sick Loved One Sees When You Are
Working on Yourself ........................................................ 38

When Treatment Fails ...................................................... 41

**Part 3 Putting Families on the Team** ........................... 43

Family's Role ................................................................... 44

So What Do Families Do? ................................................ 45

If Things Aren't Improving, Begin to
*Squeeze* Bit by Bit ............................................................. 46

*Squeeze* a Little More ......................................................... 51

*Squeeze* Fully .................................................................... 54

**Part 4 Intervention** .......................................................... **57**

What Is Intervention? .......................................................... 59

When Is Intervention Right for Your Loved One? ........... 61

Intervention Isn't Just for the "Sick" One ........................ 65

Recognizing Roles and Identities That Feed
the Sickness ........................................................................ 70

Somebody Has to Go First ................................................ 75

The Elephant(s) in the Room ............................................. 78

# PART 1

Mental Disorders, Addictions, and Insight

"There's nothing wrong with me!"

# Mental Health and Insight

Mental health works differently than the rest of health. Some argue that there should be no separation between healthcare for the mind and healthcare for the body, but nonetheless, a separation remains between how the health of the body and the health of the mind are regarded and managed. An illness of the mind can be hidden from view, and therefore difficult to understand. A person with mental illness might show no obvious outside signs of difference in a crowd of people without illness. In fact, a person with mental illness might not believe it himself or herself.

## Mental Health and Insight

Some conditions of the mind interfere with a person's ability to see that something is wrong. Mental illness can rob the bearer of insight. In fact, it's quite common for people with mental illness to question their diagnosis and/or treatment plan. Making mental illness treatment decisions with an ill mind can create an insurmountable challenge.

Josie is twenty-eight, and she was recently released from the psychiatric hospital. She started hearing voices after her miscarriage at eighteen weeks. Josie told her husband that there was someone living in the attic of their rented house, and she could hear them talking day and night up there. She said she intended to set the house on fire in order to force the intruders to show themselves. She hadn't slept in days leading up to her mental health crisis.

When Josie arrived at the hospital, she was confused about why she was being checked in to the psychiatry ward. She pleaded with her husband and her sister to address the true crisis: that strangers had invaded her residence. Instead of helping with the safety and security of her living space, they were treating her like she was crazy. She couldn't understand why they didn't believe her.

In the psychiatry unit, strangers dressed as doctors and nurses tried to drug her. Josie refused to swallow any pills. She kept to herself and vowed not to make trouble. Why her loved ones believed that these people were to be trusted, she did not know. But Josie's intuition guided her to be very cautious of the intentions of these strangers. Josie decided it was best to stop talking about the intruders in her attic. It would be wise to assure everyone that she was fine now. Perhaps that way, she would be allowed to return home.

Upon returning to her home, what's next for someone like Josie? Her husband is going to observe that something is still wrong, and he's going to want to see her get help, but Josie doesn't think she has an illness and she doesn't want the kind of help that will be offered to her.

People with serious mental illnesses don't always see the issue. In fact, many times the most serious illnesses come with a lack of insight.

Severe bipolar disorder Type I, where symptoms cycle on and off, commonly leaves people wanting to believe that they don't really have an illness. Something just went haywire for a little while—the illness won't be coming back.

People with psychotic symptoms from underlying schizophrenia or schizoaffective disorder might have delusional (false) beliefs, but insist that the beliefs are absolutely real: "The FBI is monitoring me, and you just don't believe me!"

These serious illnesses sometimes directly interfere with a person's awareness that something is wrong. An illness that distorts reality doesn't stick neatly to the territory of beliefs about the FBI; it affects beliefs about the illness itself too.

In psychiatry, this lack of understanding or belief in the illness is so pervasive, it has many names: lack of insight, treatment resistance, and anosognosia. These terms all mean one simple thing, that the person with the symptom doesn't believe that it's a symptom.

But why does a lack of insight affect so many people with mental health diagnoses? Well for one, the disease processes themselves may be to blame. If your mental health condition causes false beliefs, it makes sense that one such falsehood could be about the presence of the conditions itself. But that's not the sole underlying reason for a lack of insight about mental illness. Some conditions affect trust in other people, and some affect intuitions or the ability to read facial expressions and emotions.

Aside from the biology of mental illness, there are psychosocial factors that affect the ability to accept the illness's veracity. For starters, many mental illnesses begin right around the time a young adult is attempting to break away from his or her parents. It may be the parents or other members of the family who step in and identify that something is wrong, and this may coincide with attempts to claim independence and separate from the family to start life on one's own. When your primary goal in life is to claim independence and find yourself, it can be hard to accept anyone's claim that you've got a problem that might affect those goals. And it can be even harder to grab some control from parents just to give it back to them a short while later.

Whether it's about parents or not, few would want to accept that there is something wrong with the way you perceive reality. The idea of having a mental illness would be terrifying. What do you mean I'm not seeing reality? How can I trust you to be the judge of that, especially when my eyes and ears are telling me something different?

Having a mental illness means losing control. Not only does it mean being unable to control one's mind, it may be giving over control of other factors too. Mental illness may require taking prescribed medication. What if there are side effects and problems? And what if mental illness claims individual freedom, by requiring short-term hospitalization or long-term supervision in a living situation where someone is around to oversee behavior and response to treatment. Believing that a mental illness is real could mean relinquishing the right to live alone or make decisions most of us take for granted each day.

Even though mental illness may start at the break between childhood and adulthood, that is not always the case. And even when it is, some people struggle with lack of insight for years, or long term. What happens when she goes on for years maintaining the belief that someone is living in her home and the best plan is to set the place on fire? What happens when her family members want her to live in a supervised setting for her own safety?

Believing that an illness is real, despite personally experiencing a different reality, takes a leap of faith and trust in others. And that leap is even harder when treatments cause problematic side effects. Sure, maybe Josie was scared when she thought there were strangers in her home. But she had a plan to take charge of the situation, and that left her feeling empowered and hopeful. How will she be convinced to take a medication if, for example, it leaves her sluggish and sedated, especially if she is still holding onto the remnants of the fear that someone unwanted resides in her home? Will she even feel safe accepting those side effects, even if she trusts her husband implicitly and wants to do whatever it takes to reassure him that she is okay?

# Addiction and Denial

Just like in cases of mental illness, the presence of an addiction can leave a person without insight. Some people with addictions fail to see that they need help. The processes are essentially the same. But in the world of addiction, the terminology is often different. Instead of "lack of insight," insiders in the addiction world will often use the word "denial."

Denial is just another way to say lack of insight, but addicts choose it because it connotes personal responsibility. "You're in denial, and you need to wake up!" This approach is the preferred method in addiction, often because there is

## Addiction and Denial

a belief in personal responsibility for healing addiction. Addicts have to stop using, and to do so, they have to wake up and admit that using is a problem.

It might seem that having an addiction would be pretty obvious, and that you'd have to twist reality dramatically to miss that you have it, but just like recognizing signs of a mental illness, it's not always so simple to see signs of the disease of addiction. Imagine Maryanne, a forty-three-year old executive assistant at a big company. Maryanne is moving up the ladder in an industry that hosts a lot of parties, all of which include a full bar. Virtually everyone drinks at the parties. From time to time, someone breaks out a vial of cocaine in the bathroom at one of the parties. Everyone knows this goes on, even though nobody discusses it at work on Monday mornings. So when Maryanne started feeling lonely a few years ago and turning to a combination of alcohol and cocaine, it was easy for her to tell herself that this was no big deal. She had seen a lot of people over the years use both substances, and although she knew it wasn't "healthy" to get drunk or get high, it seemed common in her experience.

When Maryanne's husband left her five years ago, she told herself that divorce was common. When he blamed her substance use, she brushed him off as a prude who didn't understand how normal substance use could be. And when he got primary custody of the children after Maryanne had driven them home from school under the influence, she chalked it up to a biased judge in the hearing. While Maryanne was still married and her life was working well, she had plenty of resources and reasons to get help. She had her husband to support her, and to carry the burden day-to-day while she pursued treatment. Not listening to her husband's concerns has cost her more than the marriage. Not only did she miss the chance to get help; if she had gotten help early, the disease would have been easier to get under control.

Now Maryanne lives alone and all she has left is her addiction. Most of the healthy people in her life moved on, because they either couldn't stomach watching someone they loved self-destruct or because they grew furious with her lies and deceptions. If you asked Maryanne if she is an addict, she would probably laugh and say something sarcastic about how everybody has a vice, and she is just open about hers.

Maryanne's lack of insight is just as serious and just as dangerous as Josie's. In fact, they are quite similar processes. For both biologic reasons and psychosocial reasons, it can be hard for Maryanne to see that she has a problem. If she admits to the addiction, she will have to change. She will have to give up her primary coping mechanism, and she faces the risk of having no alternatives to replace the substances as her main way to deal with stress.

If Maryanne admits that she is an addict, that would mean she might have to accept that the divorce and the loss of custody of her kids were largely her fault. If she accepts she is an addict, she will then have to stop blaming the judge and her ex-husband for the estrangement from her kids, and instead she will have to allow herself to see that she is the primary culprit. Maryanne's mind has a lot of reasons to want to continue to distort the truth. If she let herself see it honestly, how would she survive?

Instead of seeing the problem for what it is, Maryanne resorts to one of the most common mechanisms an addict uses: minimizing. She tells herself, "It's not that bad." And she believes it almost completely. Sure she drinks more than her friends on the surface of it, but who knows what really goes on in their private lives? Maybe they leave the bar after only two drinks and finish off a bottle in secret at home. Maybe they secretly take a bump of cocaine before work too. Who knows?

And while she may get a nagging suspicion that she's got a problem from time to time, Maryanne doesn't want to believe it. The ramifications would be too great. She would prefer to normalize her drinking and drug use and tell herself it's what everyone else does. That's more comfortable than facing the truth. At least for now. Maryanne doesn't want to know.

Maryanne has a brother, Stevie. Stevie drinks too, but he takes a different approach to coping. Instead of denial or minimizing, Stevie is quite certain within his own mind that he has a drinking problem. He just wants to make sure no one else knows. Stevie sips off a bottle of vodka all day long. He starts in the morning with his a.m. coffee. To keep the drinking a secret, he hides bottles everywhere. He has a bottle in his desk at work and one in the glove compartment of his car. He has a couple of bottles in the garage and another in the closet where he keeps his winter clothes stored. Stevie is married, and his spouse knows Stevie drinks, but not that he drinks all day every day.

Each evening, Stevie drinks a couple of cocktails before dinner. He pours them right out in the open, even sometimes making a show of the whole procedure. "I'm having my nightly drink," he sometimes announces. But it's all an elaborate cover-up. In truth, Stevie drinks a little bit every hour or two during all of his waking moments. The publicly announced drinks are to manage his image, and nothing more.

## Addiction and Denial

People with addictions may concoct a cover-up like Stevie. They may go to great lengths to keep appearances up. Oftentimes addicts lie and manipulate. They hide the fact that their entire lives revolve around drinking. An alcoholic may find excuses to only go to restaurants that serve booze.

But why all the effort to cover up? If Stevie wants a drink, and he truly thinks that his drinking is okay, why hide it? Why not put it right out in the open? Well for one, admitting to drinking all day at work would likely lead to losing his job. So there's an incentive to keep the secret there. But at home, Stevie could come clean and tell the truth. Why wouldn't he?

Like most addicts, Stevie knows his drinking is unhealthy and he hides it because he is ashamed. Unlike remorse or regret (the feeling that you have made a mistake and need to change), shame is the feeling that you are bad or worthless, and it often comes with a fear that the problem cannot be rectified. Shame makes people feel like they are rotten apples, and that this truth will be discovered by the ones they love. And so addicts who suffer from feelings of shame may hide their addiction for fear that others will find them to be rotten if they know.

Shame is a bad player for people with addictions, and it leads to some of the very unhealthy aspects of the disease. People lie, cheat, and steal to cover up a problem they don't want anyone to know about. And they do it to protect a fragile sense that the truth is too dangerous or ugly to allow out. The secret is the only protection.

But it's not always about something as awful as shame. Some people want to continue drinking or using drugs because drinking or drug use is the way they have grown accustomed to socializing. They want to participate. They want to be included. They want to be "normal." In fact, the desire to be normal in order to fit in is the basis for a whole lot of denial or lack of insight. For folks who want to continue to drink or use socially or normally, admitting that the drinking or drug use has gotten out of control would be a way of ostracizing oneself from friends and activities.

## Addiction and Denial

Alcoholics want to be able to crack open a beer and watch the game, even when experience has shown that a single beer is not really doable for them. They want to use willpower, when addiction has already changed their brain to the point that willpower is out of the question. They have lost the power to make a choice and they drink because they cannot stop, but the truth of the addiction is too hard to bear and the denial keeps the truth at bay.

Whatever the underlying cause of a lack of insight, people with addictions and mental health conditions run the risk of doubting their diagnosis. Whether the doubt stems from the biology of the disease process or from the psychosocial aspects of accepting the disease, the end product is the same: the mind doesn't see its own limitations objectively.

# PART 2

# How the System Tries (and Fails) to Help

# Finding Help in a Broken System

To say that the mental health and addiction care systems are broken is a dramatic understatement. Care has become increasingly unavailable. As a crisis begins to build, people start searching and quickly find that there is nowhere to go. Primary care physicians are the mainstay of mental health and addiction treatment providers, even when they feel that they lack the necessary training and specialized experience to provide safe care.

Open up a telephone book and start calling mental health professionals, and you'll find that getting an appointment with a psychiatrist (a medical specialist in behavioral and mental health and addiction) takes months. So you're left with generalist care and long wait times.

If you cannot get a mounting crisis under control, you might find yourself in an emergency room, where you'll get a few tests and perhaps an assessment for a psychiatric unit, but care won't be started in most cases since ERs only provide treatments that last a few hours or days, and mental health issues span weeks, months, or years.

Thus is the need for psychiatric urgent care clinics. Increasingly, walk-in mental health treatment has become the trend to address the gaping holes in the system as noted above.

Since medical emergency rooms only provide brief care, and psychiatric emergency assessments are usually only conducted for the purpose of determining whether or not to hospitalize, immediate access to psychiatric medical care has become a necessity. Walk-in psychiatric clinics can diagnose problems and start treatment while longer-term treatment plans are being established.

At Sigma Mental Health Urgent Care in San Antonio, Texas, we start care and stabilize for up to six months while families wait for an appointment in the usual systems of care.

# Finding Help at Last

If people with illnesses affecting the mind lack insight, then how does anyone get help? For many, treatment starts when someone they love asks them to meet with a professional out of concern. Observing a change in behavior, a friend, parent, sibling, spouse, or significant other requests that the person with symptoms have an assessment.

The mental health system is often the place that handles both mental illness and addictions. Counselors, psychologists, and medical specialists in mental health are often the first line of defense for addressing any change in behavior. The process usually goes like this: Jack, an eighteen-year-old college freshman who lives at home, is brought in by his parents to the mental health clinic for an assessment. Jack has been behaving oddly. He doesn't sleep and he doesn't appear to be going to his classes, although he won't answer questions about whether he goes. Jack's parents have known him to be a responsible young man, and have been shocked by his irresponsibility and disrespect for rules lately. Over the weeks leading up to the mental health appointment, they have become worried that something is wrong with Jack. Perhaps he is on drugs or has a new onset of a mental illness.

Jack's parents share these concerns with the medical professional at the clinic, and then leave the room to allow Jack privacy. Once alone in the room, Jack says there is nothing wrong with him. He says he has been sleeping normally, and that he did miss some classes, but that's not a big deal. He says he might just drop out of college. He calls his parents "helicopter parents."

The healthcare professional is unsure what is happening with Jack. There are no overt signs that something is wrong with him, but his parents seem credible and appropriately concerned. His description of his parents as "helicopter parents" raises some questions about which version of events is accurate. Is it possible that the parents are overreacting to normal events? No treatment is started, since it's not clear what is going on. However, a follow-up appointment is scheduled for continued evaluation.

A month later Jack shows up for his second appointment alone. He is wearing dirty clothes and he is rambling, but not knowing him very well, it is still hard for the health professional to determine what is happening. Perhaps Jack is a little bit eccentric. He says he doesn't need help, he's fine, and he doesn't plan on coming for any more appointments. No call is made to the family. No follow-up is scheduled. Jack doesn't seem to think anything is wrong or want help, so until he agrees that he has a problem that requires assistance, he is released from care.

If you're reading the story above and you don't work in mental health or addiction, then you are probably appalled. Why wouldn't the medical professional call the family? Why isn't more done for people like Jack? If you work in the field or if you have been through the system as a patient or family member, then you probably see that this case is typical.

The standard model of healthcare delivery is one of collaboration. A person wants and needs help, seeks help, receives help. That's how it works. Medical professionals, and probably most especially mental health specialists, are collaborative people. We want to help people with their problems, and leave them in peace to be odd, eccentric, different, or any other way that's not the cause of a self-identified impairment. We want satisfied customers who get the assistance they are seeking. And we don't want to force people to accept treatments that they don't think they need—at least not unless the situation is an emergency.

The medical professional evaluating Jack is most accustomed to treating people with depression and anxiety, since those conditions are more common than whatever is happening with Jack.

Typical patients arrive and say, "Can you help me? I don't feel well." The health professional then works together with the person to diagnose and treat the problem. It's a very satisfying transaction for everyone involved.

Because the healthcare system works this way, finding help for your loved one who doesn't want help requires greater effort. You'll need to be part of the team when your loved one struggles with denial, not just take them and leave them to handle to appointments without your involvement.

Most often, loved ones get involved and start the process. Some start in primary care, with a known physician who looks after general health. Some find a list of mental health providers with their insurance plan. Others seek guidance from someone in their support circles—a friend, neighbor, or clergyperson. Still others go to school counselors, employee assistance programs, or community agencies.

Whatever the route, sitting down with an expert is the place to start to get help with a mental health diagnosis or an addiction. Experts may be psychiatrists and psychotherapists, counseling professionals, or people with experience who have been there.

Once you find someone, you'll probably take your loved one to meet with that expert, and you'll probably tell your story. And then the expert and loved one will take it from there.

To avoid a situation like the one with Jack, where he quit care on the second clinic visit, you will want to be more involved in care. Attending appointments and giving updates can be an important expectation to set from the beginning. Although it will probably be best if you give your loved one time alone with his therapist or doctor, it is also important that you get a chance to share information about what's happening at home. If your loved one absolutely refuses to allow you to come in to appointments, the professional will often accept a written update or a faxed note or private email from a concerned family member.

It's important that you understand that your loved one has a legal right to healthcare privacy.

You can't ask for information. The purpose of your involvement in care is solely to give accurate information, so that the therapist or doctor gets the full picture.

Treatment can fall apart when families are shut out of the treatment altogether. Rather than finding a way to involve families while also enforcing healthy boundaries to protect privacy, many clinics choose to slam the door to loved ones and cite the HIPPA privacy rules as the reason for doing so.

HIPPA does not strictly prohibit speaking with family or loved ones. Patients have a legal right to privacy, but nowhere does it state that healthcare professionals are required to refuse to listen, educate, and reassure concerned loved ones. Hurried professionals probably rationalize the use of privacy rules as an excuse to refuse to talk to loved ones of patients.

If you are a friend or family member who has arranged treatment, or who drives to appointments or pays for care, it's important to develop your own relationship with the treatment team.

Introduce yourself. Ask questions. Understand your role. Build trust with the team that extends in both directions. But don't expect to be closely involved with treatment. Know that your role is usually to sit in the waiting room, and be a resource if asked.

Be patient and let the treatment process work. Let go of any need to be in control, and instead just be supportive and present.

# Your Loved One Found Help. Now What?

When your loved one starts getting the help he or she needs, you might not know what to do with yourself. If you're like most people who facilitate getting someone into treatment, you've probably been in a state of constant worry for weeks, months, or years leading up to finding professional help.

Once treatment starts, you may find that there's not much of a role for you. Sure, you may drive to appointments or even pay for care, but once at the professional's office, you'll probably find yourself sitting in the waiting room wondering if whatever is happening in the treatment is actually helping. So what do you do in the meantime?

You're going to have to start working on yourself.

This can be a tough concept for a lot of families and loved ones. You may ask, "Why do I need to work on myself? I'm not the one with the problem here."

And while it's understandable to start out there, here's the hard truth: If you have been close enough with someone who is sick with addiction or mental illness that you led that person into treatment, then you have been living in a sick system and you also need to learn, change, grow, and become healthier.

It has been said that addiction is a family disease. In fact, this is a commonly held view throughout the addiction field. And in the same way, mental illness is also a family disease. When someone close to you is mentally ill or using substances, your world is turned upside down. Maybe you find yourself trying to rescue that person. Maybe you have become angry and pulled away.

## Your Loved One Found Help. Now What?

Maybe you've been up nights, worrying, unsure what to do. Whatever the case, the illness hasn't neatly confined itself to the so-called "sick" person in the system.

Now that treatment has begun, it will be your job to untangle yourself emotionally from the sickness of your loved one. If you've been trying to rescue, it's time to step back and focus on the things you can control in your own life. Take care of yourself. Start a fitness plan. Eat better. Adopt healthy habits. Become more self-aware and more mindful.

If you've been angry, it's time to forgive. It's time to let go of the past and move forward as a loving individual, rather than let the problems of the past get you stuck in a state of resentment and dysfunction.

If you've been worrying, it's time to trust that your loved one and your team can examine the sickness and find ways to address it. It's time to let someone else be in charge, and accept that there are some problems you cannot solve. Even more, it's time to accept that even if the sickness fails to get resolved, you were not the one in control of it.

Stepping out of the role of loved one to someone who is ill, and into the work you'll do on yourself, can be difficult. It can be hard to trust. It can be hard to let go. But this is the work a loved one must do in order to be part of the progress that treatment brings to your "sick" person.

# What Your Sick Loved One Sees When You Are Working on Yourself

You have taken your loved one to someone and asked him or her to get help. In many cases, your loved one can be skeptical that the problem is real, or that it is big enough to warrant seeking treatment.

By demonstrating that you are doing your own work on boundaries, self-care, self-awareness, or your own mental health and substance use, you move out of the role of pointing your finger at the "sick" person and demanding change from only them, and into the role of a role model for growth and change. By working on yourself, you show

## What Sick Loved One Sees When You Are Working on Yourself

that self-work is healthy, safe, and expected of everyone in the system.

Even if you're not sure you've been part of the problem, getting help and showing that you are part of the solution helps. You'll learn the language of recovery. You'll be sure to take responsibility for any unhealthy behavior you enact. You'll be the poster child for personal accountability. You'll do all the things you want to see your sick loved one do, and lead the way toward change.

By being a healthier person, you'll control your negative automatic reactions to your loved one's sickness. Instead of lashing out, you'll have thoughtful ways to deal with problems. Instead of running away, you'll learn to stay and communicate. Instead of trying to rescue, you'll learn how to hold the loved one accountable.

And you might be surprised at what you discover along the way. When you are actively working on your own role in the sickness, and your own health and behavior, you may be surprised to learn that you aren't as "right" or as "healthy" as you thought.

An added benefit of focusing on your own health is this: it helps you be patient while your loved one gets treatment with the experts you found. Rather than jumping into the treatment, trying to control what is happening there, your work on yourself keeps you occupied with plenty of your own business, so you can leave recovery to the "patient" and the team.

The team members helping you, perhaps an individual therapist or a support group sponsor, can link in with the team treating the sick person. In this way everyone can work together toward healing.

# When Treatment Fails

Unfortunately, even when you take all the right steps to get help for your loved one's mental illness or substance problem, too often, finding the treatment team doesn't lead to magical recovery.

Your loved one may refuse to participate in treatment, or drop out. He or she may distort reality, and misrepresent the facts to their expert team members, leading to treatment failure. Your loved one might drop out, and even hide that fact from you and others trying to support recovery.

When treatment falls apart, you may have to go back to the beginning and try again. You may have to wait patiently for your loved one to be willing to return to treatment, all the while continuing your own path to greater wellness and self-awareness. Or you may have to take more drastic steps like the ones outlined in the remaining chapters in this book.

# PART 3

Putting Families on
the Team

# Family's Role

While leaving families out of the nuts and bolts of mental health or addiction treatment is common practice, the fact is that treatment is more efficient and more likely to be successful when families are on the team. However, being on the team may not be what you have imagined. You don't get to decide whether your loved one takes medications, or whether he attends 12-step meetings and has a sponsor. Those are decisions for the person seeking help, under the advice of experienced and trusted professionals and people in recovery. Family members are not the primary decision makers about the day-to-day management of treatment.

# So What Do Families Do?

As a family member or supportive other, you should educate yourself and become part of the team by managing the problems at home from your side. You learn to accept responsibility for your own shortcomings and unhealthy behaviors, and you model growth. You urge your loved one to start treatment, and you urge him or her to stay in treatment. You don't do that by arguing and trying to control things; instead you nudge someone toward treatment by making yourself healthier and clearer minded, and knowing when to squeeze.

# If Things Aren't Improving, Begin to *Squeeze* Bit by Bit

Russ has agreed to get help for his dual diagnosis of bipolar disorder and cocaine and alcohol addiction repeatedly. Russ's father has known for years that Russ has had problems and needed help, and he has been very vocal in saying so. Russ started using as a teen, and it became clear over time that his most severe cycles of substance use centered on an effort to control underlying cycles with his mood. When he felt down and depressed, he would use cocaine to try and bump himself up into a higher energy and mood state. When he was "up" and unable to sleep or sit still, he would drink to try and

## If Things Aren't Improving, Begin to *Squeeze* Bit by Bit

calm himself so that he could act and feel more normal.

Russ's father has never been shy about telling his son he needed help. In fact, he is often a bit too angry and frustrated. If anything, he can't let up on the subject of Russ's problems.

When his father confronts him enough times, Russ repeatedly agrees to get help, and he begins the process of recovery for both his addiction and his mental health condition, but Russ is never willing to stick with the recovery process for very long. He starts, falls off the wagon, and quickly gives up on the promises he has made to get himself healthy.

Russ's father has researched programs, located the best doctors, facilitated connections with people in the recovery community who have been there, and basically done everything he knows how to do to get help for Russ. But he is at a loss about how to get Russ to utilize those resources and actually achieve real recovery. He doesn't know how to get Russ in treatment and have him stay there.

## If Things Aren't Improving, Begin to *Squeeze* Bit by Bit

If your loved one needs to begin a recovery process and s/he is not willing to participate, or if s/he starts treatment and then stops, you'll have to learn to stay calm and squeeze until treatment seems like a good idea.

You squeeze by facilitating less, and instead allowing the person who needs help to do more on his or her own, and accept the consequences and pressures of daily life without you there to grease the wheels and make things smooth and easy. You might need to stop paying for things. You might need to stop clearing the way. You may need to stop covering up mistakes, or making sure that your loved one always looks good to the outside world.

When you change the way you offer emotional and financial support, it places a pressure on the loved one to do something to help himself. In Russ's case, if his father can shift from talking at Russ to making him more accountable, Russ might have a reason to get healthy other than to please his dad.

## If Things Aren't Improving, Begin to *Squeeze* Bit by Bit

Russ's dad can change the story he tells to friends and loved ones that keeps Russ's addiction and mental health condition in the shadows. While he doesn't need to tell Russ's private business, he also doesn't have to keep trying to paint him in the best possible light so no one will suspect that something is wrong. When he jokes that Russ is "currently doing a prestigious internship, from home," he inadvertently makes Russ's life sound like it's going well. It might put more pressure on Russ to change if his father said, "I'll let Russ answer questions about his career plans," and people brought their inquiries directly to the source. It also might help Russ be more accountable if he applied for a job via the traditional route, instead of having his dad phone an old friend to hire Russ as a favor. When Dad makes everything a little less easy, he may be silently encouraging Russ to change what's not working in his life.

But sometimes, a little squeeze doesn't change much.

## If Things Aren't Improving, Begin to *Squeeze* Bit by Bit

Cheryl's sister has been helping her find help, and like Russ, Cheryl hasn't really stuck with a recovery plan. So Cheryl's sister began the squeeze by ceasing to clear the path or paint the pretty picture of things to the outside world. Unfortunately, six months into the little squeeze, Cheryl hasn't budged. Cheryl is living with her sister, refusing meds for her paranoia, and still using methamphetamines regularly. So now it's time to squeeze a little more. But what else can be done?

When talking doesn't change things, and clearing the path is no longer the norm, there are ways to be firmer and impose higher expectations.[*]

---

[*] Skip to Intervention if the situation is immediately dangerous or out of control.

# *Squeeze* a Little More

Cheryl's family has tried. They have incentivized getting help. Unfortunately, the pressures they placed on her just weren't strong enough to get her to accept the help she needs. Now the family feels complicit in her problem. By providing her with a place to hide from responsibility and even to use drugs, and by providing a car to go get the drugs from the dealer, as well as a smartphone to contact the dealer, Cheryl's sister feels like she has been forced to help keep her sister sick, instead of help her get the treatment she so desperately needs. But what can she do?

*Squeeze* a Little More

Families often feel that they lack the power to influence a loved one, especially when active efforts to persuade them to change have fallen on deaf ears. However, feelings of hopelessness may simply be part of the family disease. It's common to feel like you can't help, even when you can. If your sick loved one lives at home, or if you provide support, you have the power to begin removing some of the tools that fuel the illness and lack of recovery. You can turn off the internet, or encrypt access. You can take away the car, or remove the battery from the car, or hide the keys. You can hide the cell phone with the drug contacts, and opt for a low-tech flip phone or no phone at all for a while. You can limit privacy for deal-making or substance use or all manner of other unhealthy behavior by taking the door off the bedroom.

Even when your addict doesn't live in your home, if you're still helping, it may be time to peel back that help. You may need to stop paying the rent, especially if having a roof over her head is keeping her from facing the problems she needs help with. It's probably time to stop covering for her, and it's long past time to stop lying to others to paint your sick loved one in a better light or to normalize what is happening. It's also past time to stop calling the school, the employer, the landlord, or anyone who is trying to hold your sick loved one accountable for the improvements that need to happen.

# *Squeeze* **Fully**

If Cheryl's sister's efforts fail, she cannot just give up and allow the illness to continue unchecked. She will reach a point where she will fear finding her sister dead of an overdose in the house. If the illness is left to grow unchecked, drastic measures will become necessary.

Sometimes families face the difficult decision to cut off almost all support in the hopes of getting their loved one to have a reason to get help. When you reach this point, it may already be time to bring in a professional interventionist. Things are reaching a crisis point, and your loved one is not responding to your efforts to urge them into getting help.

Removing support may be the final squeeze for some. Support comes in many forms, and it not just financial. But cutting the funds that help keep your loved one afloat is sometimes necessary. Families may have to stop problem solving for the member who needs help but doesn't truly take ownership of the need to change. When you do the legwork and solve the problems caused by addiction, you may actually be interfering with the growth of your loved one in need. Solving their own problems and cleaning up their own messes make good tools for learning.

Families may have to stop intervening in relationships. It may make sense that you should try to keep your sick sibling's spouse from filing for divorce, but what if being served with divorce papers is the wake-up call that finally brings about a desire for help?

And, of course, in order to gain some traction, you may have to cut off the money. Telling your loved one that rent is contingent on being in treatment could help her accept the help she needs. But you have to be willing to follow through on this kind of threat if you make it. Hollow threats undermine trust and progress.

Reaching the point that you know you have to pull away your support in order to push your loved one into help before it's too late can be devastating. In fact, many loved ones simply cannot take these kinds of steps. Leaving someone you love homeless and hungry feels terrifying and morally wrong, and yet at the same time, making it convenient to refuse help cannot be the answer.

When you're out of options, it is time for professional intervention.

# PART 4

Intervention

# What Is Intervention?

Intervention is the process of bringing in a professional to push healing forward. Families hire interventionists when they are desperate for healing, and have exhausted their capacity to influence change with a sick loved one. Intervention is a well-established practice in addiction. Because addictions can powerfully take hold of people who suffer from them, families bring in interventionists to loosen the grip of the disease enough to urge their loved one into treatment, often in a rehabilitation center.

A similar type of intervention process can be used for people with untreated mental health conditions and a lack of insight. An experienced specialist can be brought in to consult, and to work with the family and the person suffering in order to urge the start of needed treatment.

Families hire interventionists when they are out of ideas to encourage change. They want the assistance of an experienced expert who can help facilitate turning a crisis around. Interventionists work until they achieve success. They want families to rest assured that things will turn out positively. Rich likes to say that intervention is a process, not an event. The interventionist begins by assessing the treatment needs of the individual and the family, and he continues until the needed treatments are in place and running smoothly. Intervention is not a single conversation; it is very often a long and involved series of steps, where concerned family members benefit from the experience and expertise of the interventionist to find the right programs, get the sick person to go get help, and follow along to ensure that the plan is a working success before signing off.

# When Is Intervention Right for Your Loved One?

Isaac suffers from bouts of depression and anger. He began having mood symptoms when he was a young teen, but it appeared at first that he might just be having a bumpy transition into adolescence. When he was twenty, he got arrested for threatening a neighbor during a bad episode. He tried seeing a doctor and taking medication for a while after the incident, and then stopped the treatment when he became frustrated with medication side effects. After that, he vowed to tackle the problems on his own. He didn't want or need a psychiatrist or medication.

There were additional incidences over the years, and Isaac's family would often suggest he go back to the doctor. Over time, suggestions that he needed psychiatric treatment angered him more and more. Isaac moved out, moved away from home, and took a job in construction. When Isaac had bouts of depression, he often missed work. But his skills were so valuable, his employer tried to work with him. During episodes, he started arguments with coworkers. On occasion he punched someone. He switched jobs and repeated the behaviors each time his mood cycled down.

After a dozen years of struggle, Isaac met Amber and they got married. Their life together was happy for a while, until Isaac's depression and anger began to manifest again. Amber went to Isaac's family for guidance, and they explained that he probably needed to be in psychiatric treatment but had long refused. Amber tried to talk to Isaac, and then tried to urge him into treatment. He only became enraged. She loved Isaac, and didn't want to divorce him; however, she couldn't live with a spouse so full of rage.

## When Is Intervention Right for Your Loved One?

Amber decided it was time for an intervention when she realized things were getting worse over time, and her power to influence Isaac to get help was little to none. She brought in Rich Whitman as an expert, and he met with Isaac's parents and siblings—then with Amber to understand the problems Isaac was having. The family researched suitable programs with Rich's help. They identified his need to spend time outdoors as a potential problem for keeping him in treatment for the duration. They found a place where Isaac could get help without being trapped indoors the whole time. The program was for men only centered around outdoor life, and while psychiatric assessment and treatment would be part of the program, it took a back seat to learning how to live a healthy lifestyle. The program was perfect. They had found what seemed to be the only program Isaac would agree to, and he did.

An intervention can help when you know you can't wait any longer to get help for your loved one—when the sickness has reached a tipping point, and something simply has to change.

## When Is Intervention Right for Your Loved One?

Intervention is designed to help when someone needs help but doesn't want the help—or doesn't believe they need it.

Don't wait for your loved one to finally lose everything: job, family, friends, etc. You'll have more success with intervention if you still have a bit of leverage to work with. With leverage, you can "pull" your loved one to get the treatment they need. Here's how it works:

# Intervention Isn't Just for the "Sick" One

In the process of intervention, it's not just the "sick" person in the family who receives help. In fact, Rich often says that the family can be the hardest to convince that it's time for change. When someone has a mental health condition or an addiction that reaches the point where intervention becomes necessary, the problem is greater than the individual. Living as a part of a sick system takes a toll. It affects everyone, and everyone needs to heal.

Mackenzie declined into serious mental illness over a decade, and although she refused to see a doctor or a therapist for help, she turned to illicit

## Intervention Isn't Just for the "Sick" One

drugs to try to control her symptoms. It became hard for her family members to tell the difference between effects of drug use and the baseline mental illness. When efforts to get her into treatment failed, the family accommodated. Parents stopped taking vacations because they needed to save money for emergencies, and they never knew if a crisis might happen while they were away. Siblings stayed close to home to help out. Everyone in the family system put their own lives on hold to offer support to exhausted parents.

Mackenzie's parents eventually learned about intervention, and they found the right treatment center and the right professional interventionist to get her to go. As soon as the intervention was over and Mackenzie was on her way to treatment, Mackenzie's mother started to panic. She experienced a level of anxiety she had never felt before. She feared they had made a terrible mistake, and she had the urge to go retrieve her daughter and bring her home to the status quo. While it was logically clear that a treatment center was the right step to take, emotionally it felt frightening and confusing. Mackenzie's father had a different reaction: he was filled with hope that starting treatment would be the answer to all of the family's troubles. He thought that the years of struggle were behind them, and everything was going to be bliss going forward.

Mackenzie's interventionist had warned the family that they all needed treatment to heal from the years-long sickness they lived with and adapted around. Wisely, the interventionist arranged for family therapy, starting the week after Mackenzie went into treatment.

In family therapy, each member grew to understand how unhealthy the system had become over years of sickness and chaos. They each began to understand that, in order to help Mackenzie live a healthy life after treatment, they would have to change and adapt again—to wellness. They discovered that wellness was a foreign concept and they all had some hard work ahead.

Mackenzie's interventionist knew that sending the "sick" person off to treatment wouldn't be sufficient if she were to return to the same family system she left; the system that was adapted around her sickness and making constant accommodations to keep afloat. When families grow with the treatment process, healing is bigger than just the one member of the system.

Intervention means that the identified patient gets help, and the family gets help at the same time. In this way, everyone moves forward in the same direction. Everyone heals in unison. As members of the family heal themselves, they learn that we all have our individual roles in the system that has shaped itself around a sick member. In some cases, our roles and sicknesses can even serve as seeds for the sickness to flourish.

In addiction treatment, it has long been recognized that the disease affects a family, not simply an individual. Addiction theory teaches that each member of the family takes on a role or an identity that becomes a part of the working whole of the system. And while treatment might encourage family members to clean up those identities or turn some aspects around, the identities and roles may continue on after treatment in a healthier manner.

## Intervention Isn't Just for the "Sick" One

In families where a loved one faces untreated mental illness, the same processes can be present. In some cases the identities and roles develop in response to the presence of illness, while in other cases those identities and roles may actually contribute to the development of the sickness.

# Recognizing Roles and Identities That Feed the Sickness

Here are the role identities common to the families that harbor sick members:

- the "sick" one
- savior or enabler
- scapegoat
- overachiever/hero
- lost child
- mascot

The "sick" member of the family can be a role that one adopts. A sick person may serve the system by taking attention off the problems of other individual family members, or by taking attention away from major problems in relationships such as a failing parental marriage. When a member of the family gets sick, the role actually aids the family temporarily, and in this way can become a lasting identity role for the one who adopts it.

The savior or enabler in the family is the person who smooths things over so the family can remain intact. This member of the family jumps in and saves the day when there is a crisis, and by doing so interferes with the consequences and the accountability for change of the other family members, especially the sick person. A common example is when an enabler bails out an addicted family member after a DUI. While on the surface it can seem helpful and supportive to bail a loved one out of jail, doing so can prevent that loved one from experiencing life-changing consequences of their actions and prevent their growth. This role is sometimes referred to as the "martyr" since an apparently "healthier" member of the system sacrifices himself to rescue the dysfunctional family. The enabler may not realize that the desire to rescue is often a fantasy that they can control the situation (and it never works).

The scapegoat is the member of a family system who always (or too often) takes the blame for problems in the family. The scapegoat is the family's bad guy, and all the members of the family (including the scapegoat himself) may grow to accept that he is the one to blame.

The overachiever or hero in a family system is the person who takes the attention away from the family's sickness by accomplishing amazing success. The overachiever is just that: the one who does it all and more. Often the overachiever becomes the hero because she takes on the role of caregiver in the system. She has an overdeveloped sense of responsibility that makes her take on the problems of the family at the expense of her own health and well-being.

The family's lost child is the one who withdraws in order to cope. This family member keeps a low profile and tries to stay out of the way of the illness or dysfunction.

And finally, the family mascot is the member who takes the pressure off the distressed system by drawing attention to himself, often through humor and attention-seeking behavior. This role attempts to reduce tension and stress within the system with humor and levity.

While these roles are highly pronounced in dysfunctional family systems, they may exist to varying degrees in all families. Therefore, as a family works to heal together after treatment begins, it can be healthy and helpful for each person to identify which role or roles he might be playing, and to work to untangle the dynamics of the family system from his self-identity. In this way, Mackenzie's brother might realize that he has been trying to achieve academic and professional success in order to "help" his family heal, and that he has a right to have occasional struggles without feeling like he has let everyone down.

It is also helpful for members of a family system to begin to understand that these roles aren't actually who they are as people. Roles are learned. Some of the behaviors that develop within dysfunctional families can be relinquished or softened so that they are healthier. The roles aren't even permanent; they can shift and change over time, and often do. Family members may take turns trying to rescue, or being the scapegoat, or any of the roles listed here.

As the family members each grow to understand their roles and take steps toward change, the system becomes better able to handle trouble in a healthy way. For example, the "sick" family member may begin treatment motivated to be healthy, and then decide she doesn't want to stay, pushing herself back into an unhealthy role and urging her family members to slip back into their baseline roles as well. She may call her enabling family member and say, "You have to get me out of here and let me come home." If the family enabler has already begun working toward a greater understanding of his role, he is better positioned to resist the urge to rescue. Instead of jumping in to save the day, he may work with the entire family system and the treatment team to determine the healthiest course of action.

# Somebody Has to Go First

*"We pull them with a vision rather than push them with our purpose. Then they can see a vision of a better life."*

—Rich Whitman

In some cases, families work to address their roles and identities even before the identified "sick" person is ready to begin treatment. Since the family system works as a whole, any member has the power to influence the whole group. Somebody has to start. Somebody has to get healthy first. When any family system member starts working toward becoming healthier, the system must shift to maintain balance and everyone is affected at least a little bit.

Most families who have tried to convince an addict or a mentally ill family member to get help and failed have tried to do so by pushing that person to change. But we can't push others into changing with our purpose; as Rich always says, "You have to pull them with a vision." For example, take Charles: When his mother realized he had a serious problem with marijuana, and that substance use might explain his academic problems, she urged him to change by demanding that he speak with the minister at their church. Charles's mother relied on a strong religious faith, and she credited her strong anti-drug use values to the teachings of the church. But Charles didn't want to talk to the minister. He only wanted to be allowed to live his life on his own terms.

The problem with Charles's mom's approach is that she wanted to push him in the direction of her values and beliefs. You can't push someone forward with *your* purpose. They will resist. Instead, you pull them forward with the vision that growth brings for a happier, healthier future. Your growth becomes inspired and the inspiring. Rather than tell the "sick" person he needs to be more like you, you tell him, "I'm learning so much. Come check this out!"

If a family member gets healthy first, they can get out in front of the illness. Their dysfunction is no longer a part of them, and so they have a better view. They no longer have to look around the damned elephant in the room. They say, "Come with me. I'm going this way." Then the whole system works together toward growth and change. And the patient doesn't have to do it alone.

# The Elephant(s) in the Room

The elephant in the room: the obvious, major, serious problem that everyone avoids discussing or talking about because it is uncomfortable, scary, or shameful. Families living with addiction or untreated mental health conditions usually can identify with the analogy of the elephant in the living room. The elephant = the disease no one dares speak of, lest that make it more real; the addiction and/or mental health condition.

The elephant in the room obscures everything, and it must be acknowledged and dealt with. When a family identifies the elephant and faces it, the whole system becomes healthier. They develop a process to identify the problem and move toward the solution. Because staying where they are makes it grow/increase. When there is no enabling, the illness can't survive.

A family may have more than one elephant in the room. Some of them are little elephants and can be dealt with easily. Others are the big, scary elephants like the addiction no one wants to name, or the signs of mental illness that nobody acknowledges.

When a family can see the elephants in the room and address them, that's when true healing can occur.

www.ingramcontent.com/pod-product-compliance
Lightning Source LLC
Chambersburg PA
CBHW052204110526
44591CB00012B/2067